To: Doris

from: NVCCC

Dec. 1993

MY TIME WITH GOD

Paul J. Loth

Illustrated by
Daniel J. Hochstatter

THOMAS NELSON PUBLISHERS
Nashville

Published in Nashville, Tennessee, by Oliver-Nelson Books, a division of Thomas Nelson, Inc., Publishers, and distributed by Lawson Falle, Ltd., Cambridge, Ontario.

The Bible version used in this publication is THE NEW KING JAMES VERSION. Copyright c 1979, 1980, 1982, Thomas Nelson, Inc., Publishers.

Printed in the United States of America.

Library of Congress Cataloging-in-Publication Data

Loth, Paul J.
    My time with God / Paul J. Loth.
        p.   cm.
    Summary: Presents Bible stories from the Old and New Testaments accompanied by prayers and Bible verses.
    ISBN 0-8407-9168-2 (hard)
    1. Children—Prayer-books and devotions—English. [1. Prayer books and devotions. 2. Bible stories.]   I. Title.
BV4870.L69 1992
242'.62—dc20   92-20577
                                                          CIP
                                                          AC

2 3 4 5 6 — 97 96 95 94 93 92

Contents

An Open Letter to Parents

One of the greatest gifts we can give our children is the gift of a personal time with God. There comes a time when each child must develop a personal relationship with the Lord. Getting our children started spending quiet time with God each day is the first step in that relationship.

This book is a tool to help our children spend that time with God. There are questions to guide their thinking, a story from God's Word, and help for talking to God in prayer. A key verse to memorize is provided as well.

Each lesson includes a Thinking Step, a Reading Step, and a Praying Step—all written so that children can read the lesson themselves.

The Thinking Step: Jesus always started His lessons by making people think about their life situations. When a child's devotional times begin with a moment to reflect on life, the Bible story takes on special meaning.

The Reading Step: Romans 10:17 asserts, "Faith comes by hearing, and hearing by the word of God." God's Word will not return to us void. That is why the stories included in this devotional book are Bible stories. The Lord uses every Bible story in the lives of children. The pictures in this book accompany the Bible stories in The Listening Step and will be meaningful to your children.

The Praying Step: God describes Himself as a loving father who is concerned about every detail of our lives. Teach your children to pray with that in mind, as they would converse with you, their parents. This section includes points of prayer rather than prayers to read or repeat. This is a key element in a child's relationship with God.

One more thought. I have discovered that setting aside a consistent time for devotions is perhaps the greatest key to children's success. So provide a time free of distractions and scheduling conflicts.

May this book provide your child with a tool for developing a personal relationship with our Lord.

Paul J. Loth, Ed.D.

Cain and Abel:
Worshiping God

Genesis 4:1–7

The Thinking Step

Does the Bible give any instructions for how to worship God?
What happens if you don't follow these instructions?

The Reading Step

Adam and Eve left the garden of Eden. They disobeyed God. God could not walk and talk with them as He did in the garden. Now they brought offerings to God to worship Him.

Adam and Eve had two sons. Cain was a farmer. He worked very hard to grow crops. Abel was a shepherd. He took care of the family's sheep.

Cain brought an offering to God. He brought some of his crops. Cain was proud of the crops he grew. God did not like Cain's offering. He did not like the attitude of Cain's heart. Cain wanted to show off. He did not want to worship God. Cain got angry that God did not like his offering.

Abel brought an offering to God, too. Abel did not try to show off. He just brought a young lamb and sacrificed it to God. Abel's offering pleased God. Abel wanted to worship God.

The Praying Step

Tell God you want to worship Him.

Ask Him to help you learn how to worship Him.

You shall worship the Lᴏʀᴅ your God, and Him only you shall serve.

—Matthew 4:10

Babel: Leaving God Out of the Plan

Genesis 11:1–9

The Thinking Step

Have you ever tried to talk to someone from another country?
It is hard to make people understand you when you do not speak
their language.

The Reading Step

After the Great Flood, Noah's three sons had big families. Those families grew into many nations. Everyone in the nations spoke the same language. The people traveled in groups from place to place. One day some of them had an idea. They decided to build a big city. They would build a tall tower in the city. It would reach far up into the sky. They thought the city and tower would make them very important.

God watched them start building the city. Then He saw them begin the tower. God did not like what they did. The feelings in their hearts did not bring honor to God. So God decided to stop them. He made them speak many different languages.

The people had to stop building the tower. They could not understand what anyone was saying. Then the Lord scattered the people all over the earth.

The Praying Step

Ask God to tell you what plans He has for you.
Tell Him you do not want to leave Him out of your plans.

> **Commit your way to the LORD,**
> **Trust also in Him,**
> **And He shall bring it to pass.**
> **—*Psalm 37:5***

Abram and Sarai: Trusting God

Genesis 12:1–9

The Thinking Step

Have you ever had to do something that was very hard?
Have you ever had to move to a new town?
How did you feel about leaving your friends and school?

The Reading Step

God promised Abram and Sarai that they would have a son. He said that their children and grandchildren would become a great nation. Abram and Sarai were married for many years. But they did not have any children.

Abram and Sarai lived in the city of Haran. It was a nice city. But it had one problem. The people in Haran did not worship God. They worshiped idols.

God did not want Abram and Sarai's son to grow up in Haran. He told them to pack up everything they owned. He told them to move to a new place. They obeyed God. They did not know where to go. But God said that He would show them where to move. They trusted God.

They were glad they trusted God! God kept His promises to them. They had a son named Isaac. And their grandchildren became a great nation!

14

The Praying Step

Tell God that you will do what He asks you to do.
Thank God that you can trust Him to take care of you.

Trust in the Lord with all your heart.
—*Proverbs 3:5*

Abram: Giving the Best to Others

Genesis 13:1–17

The Thinking Step

Think of a time when you and a friend wanted the same thing.
What did you do? How did you decide who won?

The Reading Step

Abram and his nephew Lot shared some land. But the land was not big enough for both of them. And Lot's workers and Abram's workers could not get along. They argued about who owned the land. What should Lot and Abram do?

Abram and Lot talked about it. Abram did not want the men to fight. He wanted everyone to get along. Abram and Lot went outside. "Look at all this land," Abram told Lot. "There is no reason to fight. You pick whatever part you want. I will take the rest." Abram knew he gave up the best land. But that was okay. He just wanted everyone to get along.

Lot and his men moved. Then God spoke to Abram. "Look as far as you can see," God said. "I will give you and your family all this land. And you will have more children and grandchildren than you can count."

Abram gave Lot the best land. But God gave Abram and his family a special place to live for many years.

The Praying Step

Ask God to help you give the best things to others sometimes.
Thank God for watching over you and helping you treat others right.

Whatever you want men to do to you, do also to them.
—*Matthew 7:12*

Abram: Believing the Promise

Genesis 15:1–6

The Thinking Step

Is it hard to wait for something someone promises to you?
Do you trust the person to keep the promise?

The Reading Step

The Lord made a promise to Abram. He promised that Abram would have a son. That had not happened yet. God told Abram to move to a new land. Abram did. But there were people there who did not like him. So sometimes Abram was in danger. Many times he thought he might be killed. One day he was sad and scared. God talked with him. God said, "I am your shield and your great reward." God wanted Abram to trust Him. God would take care of Abram.

Abram did not feel much better. He complained. God gave him the new land. But Abram did not have a son to pass it on to. Abram said, "I will die. There is only Eliezer, the man who works for me, to give my things to." The Lord told Abram again that someday he would have a son.

God told Abram to go outside and look up at the sky. The sky was full of stars. There were so many stars that Abram could not count them. God promised that someday Abram would have as many offspring as there were stars in that sky. Then Abram believed God!

The Praying Step
Ask God for patience.
Ask God to help your faith grow.
Thank Him that He means everything that is in the Bible.

Without faith it is impossible to please Him.
—Hebrews 11:6

Abraham and Sarah: Waiting for God

Genesis 16:1–3, 15–16; 17:18–21; 21:1–10

The Thinking Step

How do you feel when you are waiting for a special thing to happen?

Do you get tired of waiting?

Does God sometimes seem to take a long time to answer a prayer?

The Reading Step

God promised Abraham and Sarah that they would have a son. Sarah got tired of waiting. She told Abraham to marry her maid Hagar. In those days a man could have more than one wife. Abraham did marry Hagar. They had a baby boy. His name was Ishmael.

God still said that Abraham and Sarah would have a son. Abraham and Sarah did not believe God. They were tired of waiting for Him to keep His promise. But finally Isaac was born to Abraham and Sarah.

Sarah's plan for Abraham to marry Hagar caused a lot of trouble. Sarah was mean to Hagar and Ishmael. Ishmael's and Isaac's children fought each other for many years. Abraham and Sarah should have waited for God's plan.

The Praying Step

Ask God for patience to wait for answers to prayers.
Thank God that He hears your prayers.
Thank God that He always answers.

> **Rest in the LORD, and wait patiently for Him.**
> **—*Psalm 37:7***

Sarah: Enjoying What God Gives Us

Genesis 18:1–12; 21:1–5

The Thinking Step

Do you like to be happy?
What kinds of things make you laugh?

The Reading Step

Sarah and Abraham named their son Isaac. *Isaac* means "laughter." There were special reasons that they gave Isaac this name.

Sarah and Abraham lived in a tent in the desert. One day three men stopped by their tent. Abraham knew that they were angels from God. He gave them a cool drink. Sarah rushed around. She made a fancy dinner for them. The men talked with Abraham. One of them said, "Your wife will have a baby boy soon." Sarah heard him say this. She laughed right out loud! Sarah wanted a baby very much. But she did not think she could have one.

Sarah did have a baby. She remembered the day God made her laugh. She and Abraham named their son Isaac. She wanted everyone who heard his name to laugh with her.

The Praying Step

Thank God for one or two things He has given you.
Ask God to help you be joyful.

> **My mouth shall praise You with joyful lips.**
> **—*Psalm 63:5***

Abraham and Isaac: Passing God's Tests

Genesis 22:1–18

The Thinking Step

Do you like to take tests at school? Some tests are like tryouts. What are some things you have to try out for?

The Reading Step

Abraham had a son named Isaac. He loved Isaac very much. Abraham loved God very much too. God promised that Abraham and Sarah would have many children and grandchildren. They would become a great nation.

One day God gave Abraham a test. He told Abraham to offer Isaac as a sacrifice. This made Abraham very sad. But he did not argue with God. Abraham obeyed right away. He got things ready.

It was time to make the sacrifice. God said, "Stop. Do not hurt your son. Now I know that you love God most of all!"

Then God told Abraham, "You obeyed Me. Now I will bless you and your children and all the nations on earth."

The Praying Step

Ask God to help you when you have to take a test.
Ask God to help you trust Him.
Ask God to help you love Him most of all.

The testing of your faith produces patience.
—James 1:3

Jacob: Leaving Home

Genesis 27:41–43; 28:10–17

The Thinking Step

Do you get homesick at a friend's house?
Have you missed your friends on trips with your family?

The Reading Step

Jacob and his brother Esau fought. In fact Esau said he would kill Jacob. Their parents, Isaac and Rebekah, thought Jacob should leave for a while. They sent him to visit his uncle. Jacob traveled by himself.

Jacob walked all day. It got dark. He stopped to sleep. There was no place to lay down except on the ground. Jacob used a rock for a pillow. He looked up at the sky full of stars. Maybe he was lonely.

Jacob went to sleep. He dreamed about a big ladder. It went from earth all the way to heaven. Angels went up and down the ladder. Then Jacob saw the Lord above the ladder. God told Jacob that He would be with him wherever he went. God said He would bring Jacob back home some day.

Jacob woke up. He looked around. Everything looked as it did before his dream. But Jacob did not feel the same! "The Lord is in this place," he said. "This is the gate of heaven!" Jacob did not feel alone anymore. He thought about the dream as he walked the next day.

The Praying Step

Thank God that He knows everything that happens to you.
Thank God that He is always with you.

> **Whenever I am afraid,**
> **I will trust in You.**
> **—*Psalm 56:3***

Jacob: Paying a Price for Trickery

Genesis 29:1–26

The Thinking Step

Have people ever played tricks on you?

How did you feel?

Did you look for chances to pay them back with tricks of your own?

The Reading Step

Jacob met a beautiful woman named Rachel. He loved her. He wanted to marry her. Rachel's father was Jacob's Uncle Laban. Laban was happy to have Jacob marry his daughter. They agreed that Jacob would work for Laban for seven years. Then Laban would let Rachel marry Jacob.

The seven years passed quickly for Jacob. He could hardly wait to marry Rachel. It was time for the wedding. But Laban tricked Jacob. He made Jacob marry Leah, Rachel's older sister. Jacob wanted to marry Rachel. He had to work for Laban seven more years.

Things never got much better in that family. Even the two sisters and their children played tricks. They did not have a happy family. No one wanted to be a peacemaker.

The Praying Step

Ask God to help you forgive those who play tricks on you or treat
you unfairly.

Thank Him for forgiving you.

> **Blessed are the peacemakers,**
> **For they shall be called sons of God.**
> **—*Matthew 5:9***

Esau: Welcoming His Brother Home

Genesis 32:1—33:17

The Thinking Step

Why is it sometimes hard to forgive someone who hurts you?
Are you willing to forgive and forget even when someone owes you
    an apology?

The Reading Step

Jacob was away for a long time. Now he was going home with his family, his servants, and his livestock. Jacob knew he would see his brother again. He felt guilty about the trick he played on Esau. He heard Esau was coming to meet him with 400 men. Jacob thought his brother wanted to pay him back!

Jacob sent some of his livestock to Esau as a present. Jacob thought this would make Esau feel more friendly.

The brothers met. Jacob bowed seven times! But Esau hugged and kissed Jacob. They both shed happy tears. Esau would not accept Jacob's present. He said he had enough livestock. But Jacob insisted. Esau wanted to ride along with Jacob's group. But Jacob said the children and animals needed to travel slowly. Esau offered to leave some men to help. Again Jacob said no. So Esau planned to meet Jacob in Seir.

The Praying Step

Ask God to help you say "I'm sorry," even if you think it was not all your fault.

Tell Him you do not want to keep anger in your heart.

Love suffers long and is kind. *—1 Corinthians 13:4*

Jacob: Starting Over with God

Genesis 35:1–14

The Thinking Step

Do you make mistakes with friends?
Do you ever wish you could just start over?
Do you ever feel like giving up because you make mistakes?

The Reading Step

Jacob tried to do what God told him to do. But he made a lot of mistakes. He told God he wanted to start over. So God told him to go back to Bethel. God talked to Jacob in Bethel when he ran away from Esau. God asked Jacob to build an altar to worship Him there.

Jacob knew there would have to be some changes. He had spent a lot of time getting rich. He had not taught his family about God. Some of his family worshiped idols as their neighbors did. Jacob told them that they were going back to Bethel. He told them to throw out the idols and to clean up for the trip. They did what Jacob told them to do.

They got to Bethel. God talked to Jacob again. God gave Jacob a new name. It was Israel. *Israel* means "One who goes with God." Jacob had made mistakes. But now he was starting over. Jacob was happy. He built an altar to worship God.

The Praying Step

Thank God that He does not give up on us when we make mistakes. Ask God for His help to do things right.

> **Even so we also should walk in newness of life.**
> **—*Romans 6:4***

Joseph: Thinking About Others' Feelings

Genesis 37:1–11

The Thinking Step

Do you know what bragging means?
Have you ever been proud of something and told everyone about it?
Do you try to think how others feel when you are telling good news?

The Reading Step

Jacob had twelve sons. The youngest son was named Joseph. Joseph was Jacob's favorite. Jacob gave him presents that the other boys did not get. Joseph's brothers were jealous of him. They felt sad because their father liked Joseph the most.

Joseph helped his brothers take care of the sheep. Once he told his father some bad things that his brothers did. That did not make his brothers very happy.

Then Joseph had two dreams. In the dreams his family bowed down to him. He was more important than they were. Joseph told his brothers all about the dreams. They did not like the dreams. They did not want to bow down to Joseph. Even Joseph's father thought he was bragging. Soon after this some bad things happened to Joseph. He had to learn to be kind and forgiving.

The Praying Step

Ask God to help you think about how other people feel.
Tell God you want to help others, not hurt them.

Be kindly affectionate to one another with brotherly love.
—*Romans 12:10*

Joseph: Trusting God in Times of Trouble

Genesis 37:3–4, 12–28; 45:4–7

The Thinking Step

Do you know what trust means?
How would you feel if someone you trusted hurt you?

The Reading Step

Joseph's brothers did not like him. They were jealous because their father liked Joseph better than he liked them.

One day Joseph's brothers sold him to some traders. The traders wanted to make Joseph work as a slave in Egypt. The brothers told their father that a wild animal ate Joseph.

God helped Joseph while he was in Egypt. When the king of Egypt had a dream, God told Joseph what it meant. And Joseph told the king. That made the king happy! He put Joseph in charge of many things.

Many years later Joseph's brothers came to Egypt. They did not have any food at home. But Joseph was able to help them!

The Praying Step

Thank God that He is in charge.
Thank God that He takes care of you when things are hard.

We know that all things work together for good to those who love God.

—*Romans 8:28*

Joseph: Loving Your Enemies

Genesis 37:25–28; 39:20; 41:1–41, 57; 42:1–3; 45:1–11

The Thinking Step

Would you help someone who was mean to you?

Bad things happen. But sometimes what we think is bad turns out to be good. Has this ever happened to you?

The Reading Step

When Joseph was 17, his brothers sold him as a slave. Joseph was taken to Egypt and put in prison.

Pharaoh had a dream about a terrible famine that was coming. But God was with Joseph. God told Joseph what the dream meant. And Joseph told Pharaoh to begin storing up food right away. Pharaoh was happy. He put Joseph in charge of collecting crops.

People in other countries went to Egypt to buy food. Joseph's brothers went to buy food, too. They made many trips before Joseph told them who he was. They were afraid. But Joseph said God had sent him there to save their lives. He hugged them and told them he would provide for them.

The Praying Step

Ask God to make you a forgiving person.

Thank God that He turns hurtful things into ways He can show His love!

Love your enemies, do good to those who hate you.
—*Luke 6:27*

Pharaoh: Saying No to God

Exodus 7:1—12:32

The Thinking Step

When your parents tell you to do something, do you obey right away? What would happen if you told your parents no?

The Reading Step

God's people lived in Egypt for a long time. They were slaves. God sent Moses and Aaron to Pharaoh. They told him to let the Israelites go free. Pharaoh said no. Moses told Pharaoh God would punish him.

God sent many problems to the Egyptians. All their water became unfit to drink. There was a big hailstorm. Then there were swarms of flies everywhere. After that frogs covered the ground. The Egyptians' cattle died. Their crops were killed. After each problem Moses asked Pharaoh to let God's people go. Each time Pharaoh said no. God gave Pharaoh one last chance to obey. But he said no again. That night the oldest child in every Egyptian home died. Even Pharaoh's son died!

Pharaoh did not argue anymore. He told Moses to take the Israelites and go. Pharaoh paid a terrible price for saying no to God.

The Praying Step

Ask God to forgive you for times when you did not obey right away.
Thank Him for strength to help you obey.
Thank Him for His love.

It is God who works in you both to will and to do for His good pleasure.

—*Philippians 2:13*

God: Showing His People the Way

Exodus 13:20–22

The Thinking Step

How would you know where you were going without roads or maps?

How do you know God is with you?

Are there times when you feel really close to God? When?

The Reading Step

Many Israelites left Egypt with Moses. He was their leader. During the day they marched in groups. They made sure no one got lost. When it got dark they usually camped. But sometimes they traveled all night and rested during the day. Moses had no maps. And there were no highways. How did the people find their way?

God traveled with them. In the daytime everyone saw His presence in a cloud. The cloud went ahead of them. At night the cloud became a fire above them. It kept them safe from their enemies. It also showed them where to go and when to stop.

In the morning or at night, Israelite boys and girls could look up at the sky and know God was with them!

42

The Praying Step

Thank the Lord that He has promised to be with you always.

Ask Him to help you feel close to Him at play, at school, at home, and at church.

> **You will show me the path of life;**
> **In Your presence is fullness of joy.**
> **—*Psalm 16:11***

The Israelites: Trusting God's Provision

Exodus 16:1–8

The Thinking Step

Do you complain if things do not go the way you want?
Do you ever want something that you do not have?
Do you ever worry that God will not give you what you need?

The Reading Step

God helped Moses bring the Israelites out of Egypt. Now they were not slaves anymore. The king's army from Egypt tried to catch them. But God opened the Red Sea. The Israelites walked through on dry ground. The army of Egypt drowned in that sea.

But now the Israelites forgot all of God's miracles. They had walked in the desert for a long time. The food was gone. The Israelites were hungry. They got angry with Moses. They said Moses led them to the desert to starve.

God did another miracle. Each night at bedtime the ground was bare. Each morning the Israelites found food on the ground. God gave them manna. Manna was small and round like little cookies. Every person had enough to eat. God took care of the Israelites.

The Praying Step

Ask God to help you not complain.
Thank God for each good thing He gives you.
Ask God to help someone you know who needs something.

My God shall supply all your need according to His riches in glory by Christ Jesus.

—*Philippians 4:19*

Moses: Spending Time with God

Exodus 19:18–20; 24:18

The Thinking Step

Have you ever been at the top of a mountain?
What was it like?
How did you feel?

The Reading Step

Moses was important. He was special to God. Moses loved God very much. God and Moses enjoyed being together. One day God told Moses to go up to the top of the mountain.

So Moses climbed to the top of the mountain. Smoke covered the top of the mountain. And the mountain quaked. Moses and God talked to each other. God told Moses what to tell the people. Moses spent over a month talking to God on the top of the mountain. Moses enjoyed spending time with God.

The Praying Step

Tell God you want to spend more time with Him.

Ask God to help you find more time to talk with Him.

Pray without ceasing.   —*1 Thessalonians 5:17*

Caleb and Joshua: Believing God Is Able

Numbers 13:1–3, 25–33

The Thinking Step

What are some promises God made to His people?
Does God always keep His promises?

The Reading Step

God promised His people that they would live in the land of Canaan. The people had been traveling for a long time. They were ready to go into their new land. Moses, their leader, sent twelve men into Canaan to see what the land was like.

Ten of the men said there were cities with big walls and big armies. They told God's people they would lose.

Caleb and Joshua did not agree with their friends. They also said there were big walls and big armies. But they told God's people they would win.

But the people were afraid. They did not believe God would keep His promise to give them the land of Canaan. So they lived in tents in the desert for the next forty years.

The Praying Step

Thank God for the promises He has made in the Bible.
Ask God to help you always to believe He means what He says.

For with God nothing will be impossible.
—*Luke 1:37*

Moses: Anger Does Not Honor God

Numbers 20:1–12

The Thinking Step

Have you ever been angry with a friend or brother or sister?

Has someone been angry with you?

How do you feel when others say angry things to you?

The Reading Step

Moses tried to do everything God asked. He led the Israelites out of Egypt. They were not slaves anymore.

They walked in the desert for a long time. They did not have any water for themselves or the animals. The Israelites said it was Moses' fault. They said, "Why did you bring us out to the desert to die?"

God told Moses to call all the Israelites together. They stood in front of a big rock. God told Moses to speak to the rock. Then water would come out of the rock.

Moses did what God told him to do. The Israelites came and stood in front of the rock. But then Moses got angry. He thought the people were ungrateful. He said, "I will make water come out of this rock. Will that make you happy?" Then Moses hit the rock with his stick two times.

Water came out of the rock. God's promise was true. But God was not happy with Moses. He was sad that Moses got angry.

The Praying Step

Ask the Lord to help you get rid of angry feelings.
Thank Him for the peace and love He gives.

Let the peace of God rule in your hearts.
—*Colossians 3:15*

Balaam: Caring Too Much for Money

Numbers 22:1–35; 24:10; Jude 11

The Thinking Step

Some people will do anything for money. What would you do for money? Would you do something that God says is wrong?

The Reading Step

Balaam was a prophet. He spoke to the people for God. But Balaam cared too much for money.

King Balak saw the Israelites defeat the Amorites. God helped the Israelites. King Balak was afraid. He said he would pay Balaam to curse the Israelites. God stopped Balaam. So Balak offered Balaam more money. Finally God said Balaam could go. But Balaam could say only what God told him to say.

Balaam rode down the path on his donkey. He could not see an angel blocking the path. The donkey saw the angel and stopped. Balaam hit the donkey. He shouted at her to go. Then the Lord let Balaam see the angel. God told Balaam that the donkey saved his life.

Balaam spoke to the people of Israel. All he could do was bless them. Balak was not happy.

The Praying Step

Tell God you want to do your best for Him.
Ask Him to help you not care too much for money.

The love of money is a root of all kinds of evil.
—*1 Timothy 6:10*

Achan: Admitting When You Do Wrong

Joshua 7:1—8:2

The Thinking Step

If you do something you know is wrong and you get caught, what do you do?

Do you try to cover up your wrong action?

The Reading Step

God helped the Israelites win the battle of Jericho. The people of Jericho worshiped idols. So God told Joshua to burn everything the people left in the city. But Achan did not obey. Achan took some things from Jericho back to camp. He buried them under his tent.

Later Joshua led the Israelites into another battle. Everyone thought this battle would be easy to win. But it was not easy. In fact, the Israelites ran for their lives. Joshua felt bad. He asked God what happened. God told him that someone took things from Jericho. God could not help them fight when someone sinned. Joshua found out that Achan stole things and buried them. Achan said only that he took the things because he wanted them. Achan and his family were punished.

The Praying Step

Ask God to help you admit when you do wrong.
Thank Him that He will always forgive you.

Let the words of my mouth and the meditation of my heart
Be acceptable in Your sight.
—*Psalm 19:14*

Samson: Keeping Promises

Judges 16:4–31

The Thinking Step

Have you ever made a promise that you could not keep?
How did you feel when you broke the promise?

The Reading Step

Samson was a Nazirite. He promised to serve God. He let his hair grow long as a sign of this promise. This was a secret between God and Samson. Samson was very strong and brave.

The Philistines wanted to know why Samson was so strong. They talked to Samson's friend Delilah. They said, "We will give you money if you find out what makes Samson so strong."

Delilah begged Samson to tell her the secret of his strength.

Samson teased her and made up stories. At last Samson got tired of Delilah's questions. He told her the secret of his strength was the promise never to cut his hair.

Samson went to sleep. Delilah had a man cut his hair. Then the Philistines came and captured Samson. He had no strength to fight. He broke his promise to God. Later, Samson's hair grew long again. He killed the Philistines.

The Praying Step

Thank God that He always keeps His promises.
Ask God to forgive any promises you have broken.

Put on the whole armor of God. —*Ephesians 6:11*

Ruth: Being Loyal

Ruth 1:1—2:23; 4:13–17

The Thinking Step

Are you a loyal friend?
Can your friends count on you no matter what?

The Reading Step

Naomi and her husband Elimelech moved to Moab. Soon their sons grew up. They each married girls from Moab. Then Elimelech and both sons died.

Naomi was left with her two daughters-in-law. They were Orpah and Ruth. Naomi decided to go back to Bethlehem. Orpah went home. But Ruth stayed with Naomi. She would go wherever Naomi went. Naomi's family would be her family. And she would worship God as Naomi did.

Ruth and Naomi moved back to Bethlehem. They were poor. In those days farmers left some grain in the field. The poor people came and picked it up. So Ruth gathered grain from the field of Boaz. He was a kind and rich man.

Boaz and Ruth met. He knew she left her home to be with Naomi. Boaz knew that Ruth worshiped God. He asked her to marry him.

The Praying Step

Tell the Lord you will follow Him, even if you have to say good-bye to someone or something.

Thank Him for loving you, even before you knew Him.

> **Blessed are those who keep His testimonies,**
> **Who seek Him with the whole heart!**
> **—*Psalm 119:2***

The Israelites: Not Choosing God's Way

1 Samuel 8:1–22

The Thinking Step

Have you ever done something bad because your friends were doing it? Why is it hard to be different from everyone else?

The Reading Step

God did some great miracles for His people. He brought them out of Egypt. He gave them food from heaven. He gave them a new land. He helped them fight their enemies.

The Israelites should have been happy. But they complained. The Israelites wanted a king to lead them. All the countries around them had kings. They wanted to be like their neighbors. Samuel tried to warn the Israelites. He told them a king would want the young men to be in the army. A king would want the young women to work in his palace. A king would take the people's crops and animals for himself.

The people did not listen to Samuel. They wanted their own way. They wanted a king. Finally the Lord told Samuel to let them have a king. The people rejected God, not Samuel.

The Praying Step

Tell the Lord you want Him to be in charge of your life.
Thank Him for people who help you know His way better.
Ask Him to help you choose His way.

Be imitators of God as dear children.   —*Ephesians 5:1*

Saul: Making Excuses for Disobeying

1 Samuel 15:1–23

The Thinking Step

Do you ever not do a job your parents give you?
Do you give an excuse for not doing the job?
How do your parents feel when you give excuses?

The Reading Step

The Amalekites fought against God's people. God said it was time to stop them. He told King Saul to destroy them and everything they owned. Saul was not to leave one Amalekite alive.

Saul obeyed part of God's command. He fought the Amalekites. But he let the king live. Saul's men took things that belonged to the Amalekites. Saul only destroyed the things that no one wanted. Samuel asked Saul why he did not obey God. Saul said it was the soldiers' fault. They wanted to keep the things.

Samuel said, "You did not obey God. He will not let you be king anymore."

The Praying Step

Ask God to help you do the things He asks.
Tell God you will try to obey Him.

The entrance of Your words gives light.
—Psalm 119:130

Samuel: Choosing for the Right Reasons

1 Samuel 16:1–13

The Thinking Step

Do you ever want to be with people just because they look good?
Are you ever disappointed because they are not nice?

The Reading Step

Samuel helped the Israelites understand and obey God's laws. But the people wanted a king. God chose Saul to be the king. He was tall and handsome. He looked like a good king.

But Saul did not obey God. So God told Samuel that He would choose a new king.

God sent Samuel to visit a man named Jesse. Seven of Jesse's sons came to Samuel. Each one was tall and handsome. Samuel wondered which one God wanted to be king. But God looked at their hearts. And God did not choose any of them.

Jesse had one more son. David was the youngest son. He took care of the sheep. David came to Samuel. God said, "This is the one I have chosen!"

The Praying Step
Ask God to help you want to please Him.
Tell God you want to please Him.

Create in me a clean heart, O God,
And renew a steadfast spirit within me.
—*Psalm 51:10*

David: Giving Way to Sin

2 Samuel 11:1–5, 14–17; 12:1–14, 24; Psalm 51:1–4

The Thinking Step

How do you feel after you do something wrong?

Do your parents get angry with you?

Does God stop loving you when you do wrong?

The Reading Step

God chose David to be the king of Israel. He chose David because David wanted to serve God. But sometimes David made bad choices. He did not do what God wanted.

David made a bad choice with Bathsheba. Bathsheba was a beautiful woman. But she was married to a man named Uriah. David took Bathsheba from Uriah. Then he told the leader of his army to make sure Uriah died in a battle. God sent His prophet Nathan to talk to David. He told David that God would punish him for his sins.

David knew that what he did was wrong. He told God he was sorry. God forgave David. God did not stop loving David. But David's sin caused many problems years later.

Bathsheba and David got married. They had a baby boy named Solomon. Solomon grew up to be a good king.

The Praying Step

Ask God to make you strong enough to say no to wrong things.

Tell God when you do something wrong.

Thank God that He never stops loving you.

[You] are kept by the power of God through faith for salvation.

—*1 Peter 1:5*

Solomon: Asking for Wisdom

1 Kings 3:5–13

The Thinking Step

If you could have anything you wanted, what would you ask for?
Why would you choose that?
Do you think you will choose something different when you are older?

The Reading Step

Solomon was king of Israel. One day God told Solomon he could have anything he wanted. Solomon said, "I am a young king. Many people come to me for help and advice. I want to be able to tell the difference between good and evil."

This answer made God happy. He said, "You did not ask to be rich or famous. So I will give you a wise and understanding heart. I will also give you what you did not ask for. You will be rich and famous too."

Solomon was king of Israel for forty years. He lived in a beautiful palace. He was very rich. He built a beautiful temple for God. People came from all over the world to talk to him. The book of Proverbs contains some of Solomon's wise sayings. Solomon is one of the wisest men who ever lived.

The Praying Step

Thank God for your mind.
Ask Him to help you put good things in your mind.
Ask Him for wisdom to make good choices.

> If any of you lacks wisdom, let him ask of God, who
> gives to all liberally and without reproach.
>
> —*James 1:5*

Solomon: Building the House of the Lord

1 Kings 5:1–18; 6:11–14

The Thinking Step

Home is a special place to be. The people at home love you.
The place you go to worship God is His home. Are you glad to have a
place to worship God? Do you feel good when you are there?

The Reading Step

Solomon's father, King David, wanted to build a house for God. It would be a beautiful place. God's people could go there to worship Him. God told David that Solomon would build it. So David gathered everything that Solomon would need. Solomon was excited to finish the project that his father cared so much about.

The house Solomon built for God was called a temple. Solomon used 30,000 workers to dig the stones he needed. They also cut many logs and floated them in by sea. Beautiful carvings were in each room of the temple. Everything was covered with gold. Solomon wanted people to see the temple and remember God. It took seven and a half years to build the temple.

Many years later Jesus often went to the temple. He called it "My Father's house."

The Praying Step

Thank God for all the things that remind you of Him.
Thank God for special places where you can go to learn more about Him.

I was glad when they said to me,
"Let us go into the house of the LORD."
—*Psalm 122:1*

71

Elisha: Wanting God's Help

2 Kings 2:9–15

The Thinking Step

When was the last time you needed help with something?
What did you do? Who helped you?
Think of a time you needed help from God.

The Reading Step

Elijah was a special person. God gave Elijah a special message to tell people. We call Elijah a prophet. Elisha followed Elijah. God gave Elisha a special message, too.

God's job for Elijah was finished. It was Elisha's turn to tell people God's message.

"What do you want me to give to you before I leave?" Elijah asked Elisha. Elisha thought for a moment. "I want a double portion of your spirit." Elisha meant he wanted more of God's help than even Elijah had.

Soon Elijah went to heaven to be with God. Elisha looked up into heaven after him. Then he saw Elijah's coat. Elisha put it on. Now he could do God's work. He could give people God's message. Elisha had God's help.

The Praying Step

Talk to God about something difficult you have to do.
Ask God to help you do it.

With men it is impossible, but not with God.
—*Mark 10:27*

Josiah: Following God's Rules

2 Kings 22:1–10; 23:1–22

The Thinking Step

What do most eight-year-olds spend their time doing?
Do you know any eight-year-old kings?

The Reading Step

Josiah became king when he was only eight years old. He wanted to please the Lord. Josiah used King David as an example of how to live for God.

The house of the Lord was not used for many years. It needed many repairs. Josiah hired workers to fix up the temple. While they worked, the high priest found something important. He found the Book of the Law. The book had rules for living that God gave to Moses. A scribe brought the book to King Josiah. He read some of the rules. The young king was shocked. The people of Israel were not following God's rules. Josiah thought God was angry at the people!

Josiah called all the people together. He read God's rules to them. Josiah told God he would follow the rules. He threw all idols out of the temple. Josiah punished people who taught others to worship idols.

Then Josiah led the people in a big celebration.

The Praying Step

    Tell God you want to follow His rules.

    Ask Him for courage to live the way He wants you to live.

    Thank Him for His help.

> **Even a child is known by his deeds,**
> **Whether what he does is pure and right.**
> **—*Proverbs 20:11***

The Wise Men: Accepting God's Invitation

Matthew 2:1–12

The Thinking Step

Do you like to go to birthday parties?
Have you ever gone to a party for someone else and received a gift?

The Reading Step

God's Son, Jesus, was born in Bethlehem. God wanted everyone to know about His gift to the world. Some wise men lived in another country. God sent them a special invitation. God put a big star in the sky. The wise men saw it. They knew God's Son was born.

The bright star led the wise men on their trip. The wise men took gifts with them for the baby. They took gold, frankincense, and myrrh.

Soon the wise men were in Jerusalem. They asked everyone where to find the child. They wanted to worship Him.

That night the wise men saw the star again. It led them to Bethlehem. They found young Jesus. They gave Him their gifts and worshiped Him.

The Praying Step

Thank God for His wonderful gift of Jesus.
Tell Him that you want to tell others about His gift.

> **For God so loved the world that He gave His only begotten Son.**
>
> *—John 3:16*

Joseph: Following God's Directions

Matthew 2:13–23

The Thinking Step

Do you do what your teacher tells you to do?
That is called following directions.
Have you ever followed directions on a package?
You must do everything the directions say. Then the thing you are
making will come out right.

The Reading Step

God sent His Son to live in a family on earth. He trusted Joseph to take care of Jesus. God knew Joseph would follow His directions.

Once God sent an angel to Joseph. The angel told Joseph to leave Bethlehem. He told Joseph to take Mary and baby Jesus to Egypt. There was a bad king who wanted to hurt Jesus. They left Bethlehem that night.

A few years passed. Then Joseph got new directions from an angel. This time the angel said they could go home. The bad king was dead now. Joseph took his family back to Galilee. They lived in the town of Nazareth. Jesus lived there until He was grown up and ready to do the work God had for Him.

The Praying Step

Thank God for the Bible. It has His directions in it.
Ask God for help to follow His directions.

> He leads me in the paths of righteousness
> For His name's sake.
> —*Psalm 23:3*

The People of Jerusalem: Cheering for a King

Matthew 21:1–9

The Thinking Step

Do you like the excitement of parades? Flags. Decorations. Prancing horses. Marching bands. Cheering.

What are some things that make you want to cheer?

People in Jerusalem shouted, "Hurrah for King David's Son!"

The Reading Step

Jesus spent the night with His friends in Bethany. He was getting ready to visit Jerusalem for the last time. He stopped at the Mount of Olives. He told His disciples to bring Him the donkey and colt from the next village. The animals were tied up outside the owner's house. Jesus told the disciples to say "The Lord has need of them" if anybody asked what they were doing.

Everything went as planned. The disciples put their coats over the colt's back. Jesus took His seat. A large crowd started to follow them. Some people threw down their coats to make a soft carpet. Some people spread tree branches across the dusty road. People shouted, "Hosanna!"

The Praying Step

Thank God for giving you things to cheer about.
Thank God for helping you to do what He wants.

> Behold, I have come—
> In the volume of the book it is written of Me—
> To do Your will, O God.
> —*Hebrews 10:7*

Judas: Betraying the Savior

Matthew 26:14–16, 47–50; 27:1–5

The Thinking Step

Do your friends ever tell lies about you or get you in trouble?
If they do, you know how it feels to be betrayed.
Do you betray Jesus with your words or your actions?

The Reading Step

Jesus called the twelve apostles to be with Him. He included Judas. Jesus healed sick people. He hushed the stormy winds and waves. He fed 5,000 hungry people. He made Lazarus live again. Judas was there each time. One night Judas led Jesus' enemies to a garden. Jesus was there. Judas kissed Jesus. And the crowd arrested Him.

Judas betrayed Jesus for 30 pieces of silver.

The crowd took Jesus to Pontius Pilate. Then Judas changed his mind. He tried to give back the silver. He told Jesus' enemies he did wrong. Judas felt guilty. Jesus' enemies did not care. So Judas threw down the silver. Then he went away and hanged himself.

The Praying Step

Tell Jesus you want to be His true and loving friend.

Ask Him to help you not to be embarrassed or afraid to let your friends know He is your Savior.

The wages of sin is death, but the gift of God is eternal life in Christ Jesus our Lord.

—*Romans 6:23*

The Risen Christ: Giving Final Instructions

Matthew 28:18–20; Acts 1:8–9

The Thinking Step

Do your parents ever leave you for the evening?
They usually give you some final instructions, right?

The Reading Step

Jesus finished His work on earth. Now He could go back to heaven. His disciples did not want to say good-bye. They would miss Jesus very much. He promised to send the Holy Spirit to help them. He promised that someday He would come back for them. He also gave them an important job to do.

"Go into all the world and preach the gospel to everyone," He told them. Jesus wanted the whole world to know how much He loved them. Someone had to tell them.

Then a cloud covered Jesus. He went up to heaven in the cloud. The disciples did what Jesus asked them to do. The book of Acts in the Bible tells about some of them. Each of the disciples shared the news of Jesus' love with others.

84

The Praying Step

Tell the Lord you would like to tell others about Him.

Pray for a missionary who is telling about Jesus in another part of the world.

You shall be witnesses to Me. *—Acts 1:8*

The Paralyzed Man: Bringing a Friend to Jesus

Mark 2:1–12

The Thinking Step

Do you try to help friends with their problems?
Do you share with them how God cares about our problems?

The Reading Step

Jesus went to Capernaum. The news that He was in town spread quickly. Soon the house where Jesus stayed filled with people.

Four men went to the house. They took a friend. He could not walk. So they carried him on a stretcher. They finally got to the house where Jesus was. It was crowded. They could not even get in the door. But the four men wanted Jesus to heal their friend.

They had to find a way to get him to Jesus. The four friends climbed up to the roof of the house. They made a big hole in the roof. Then they lowered their friend through the hole. He came down right in front of Jesus!

Jesus saw how much these men wanted their friend to be healed. So He said to him, "Son, your sins are forgiven." Then Jesus told the man to pick up his stretcher and walk. The man could walk!

The Praying Step

Ask God to help your faith grow.
Ask Him to help you bring friends to Jesus.

Ask, and it will be given to you; seek, and you will find; knock, and it will be opened to you.

—*Matthew 7:7*

The Disciples: Learning from a Little Child

Mark 9:33–37

The Thinking Step

Do you know someone who always wants to be first in line?
Do you know someone who always wants to be the first one chosen?
Do you like to be around this person?

The Reading Step

Jesus and His disciples walked to Capernaum. The disciples argued about which of them was the most important. Finally they got to Capernaum. Jesus asked them what they argued about. They did not want to tell Him. They knew He would not like it. They did not have to tell Him. He already knew!

Jesus called all the disciples together. He told them how to be the most important. The most important person was the one who did things for others. He was a servant. He might feel like he was always last.

Then Jesus called a little child to Him. The disciples thought children were not important. Jesus said an important man welcomes children. Anyone who welcomes one child in Jesus' name receives Jesus.

The Praying Step

Thank Jesus that He did not want to be the most important.
Thank Him for coming to be your Savior.
Thank Him for caring about children.

Let this mind be in you which was also in Christ Jesus.
—*Philippians 2:5*

The Disciples: Letting Little Children Come to Jesus

Mark 10:13–16

The Thinking Step

Do grown-ups mind if you interrupt when they talk?
Does Jesus care as much about children as He does about grown-ups?

The Reading Step

Jesus spent a lot of time talking to people. He was never too tired to teach the people or to answer their questions.

One time some mothers brought their small children to see Jesus. His followers, the disciples, stopped the mothers. They said, "Jesus is too busy with the grown-ups. He does not have time for little children."

Jesus heard this. It made Him unhappy. He said, "Let the little children come to Me. Do not send them away. Grown-ups who want to come to God must trust Him like a little child does."

Jesus took time to talk with each small child. He asked God to bless each one. The mothers were happy! They hurried home to tell everyone what had happened.

The Praying Step

Thank God that He cares about everyone.
Thank Him that you are His child.

> Do not marvel that I said to you, "You must be
> born again."
>
> —*John 3:7*

Peter: Knowing Forgiveness

Mark 14:27–31, 66–72; John 21:15–17

The Thinking Step

What if someone accused you of something you did not do?
What if your friends knew that you were not guilty but did not say anything?
Would you forgive your friends?

The Reading Step

Jesus' time on earth was nearly over. He warned His disciples that one of them would betray Him. Then the rest of them would run away. Peter said he would never do that. Jesus said, "Before the rooster crows twice, you will deny Me three times."

That night Jesus was arrested. He had to go in front of some leaders. They were very mean to Him. Peter sat by a fire in the courtyard. Some people said they had seen Peter with Jesus. Peter was afraid. Three times he said that he did not even know Jesus. Then Peter remembered what Jesus had said. Peter was sad. He went off by himself and cried.

God raised Jesus from the dead. Then Peter talked with Him. Jesus knew Peter was sorry for saying he did not know Jesus. Jesus forgave Peter. Then Jesus gave Peter a special job. Jesus wanted Peter to teach people about Him.

The Praying Step

Ask God to help you be brave enough to take a stand for Him.
Thank Him that He forgives you when you do not take a stand for Him.

> **Your word I have hidden in my heart,**
> **That I might not sin against You.**
> **—Psalm 119:11**

Jesus: Taking Our Place

Mark 15:24–37

The Thinking Step

Have you ever been blamed or punished for something that was not your fault?

Did you feel angry?

Would you ever ask to be punished instead of your brother or sister?

The Reading Step

Do you know why Jesus died? Isaiah 53:5–6 says we were like sheep. We wandered away from God. We did what we wanted to do. And God put our sins on Jesus.

Jesus, the Good Shepherd, gave His life for the sheep. Jesus was hurt and bruised for the wrong things we do. That is how He saved us.

God is holy. He cannot just forget about sin. It has to be punished. But God loved sinners very much. He sent His Son into the world to save sinners. Jesus took the punishment for our sins. So God forgives us. He makes us new, as though we had never sinned!

The Praying Step

Tell Jesus you need Him to be your Savior.
Thank Him for the new life He gives you.
Thank Him for promising to be your Friend and Shepherd.

While we were still sinners, Christ died for us.
—Romans 5:8

Mary and Elizabeth: Being Happy for Others

Luke 1:5–56

The Thinking Step

When good things happen to friends, are you happy for them? Being happy is more fun when you can share it with a friend.

The Reading Step

Elizabeth and Zacharias were married a long time. Mary and Joseph were engaged to be married. Elizabeth and Mary were cousins. But Elizabeth and Mary did not get to see each other very often.

Elizabeth and Mary had exciting news to share. Elizabeth and Zacharias were going to have a baby. An angel told them God would give them a son. They were to name him John. Elizabeth and Zacharias waited a long time for a child. They were happy!

Mary was going to have a baby, too. The angel Gabriel appeared to Mary. He told her God had chosen her to be the mother of God's Son. His name would be Jesus.

Mary hurried to see Elizabeth. She wanted to share her happy news. They praised God together.

The Praying Step

Thank God for all the good things He does for you.
Ask Him to help you be happy with your friends.

Rejoice with those who rejoice. —*Romans 12:15*

Mary: Growing to Fit into God's Plan

Luke 1:26–38

The Thinking Step

Have you ever watched something grow from a tiny seed to a big plant?
Who planted the seed?
What plans did that person have for the full-grown plant?

The Reading Step

Mary was a young Jewish woman. She was a lot like others her age. But one thing was special about Mary. Mary tried to please God by the way she lived. She loved God very much.

One day an angel went to see Mary. The angel told her that she would have a baby boy. Mary's baby would be very special. He would be God's Son. The angel said not to be afraid. This was happening because God was happy with Mary. Mary said that she would do what God wanted.

God knew Mary would be a good mother for His Son, Jesus. She would be kind and loving. She would teach Him all He needed to know. God knew Mary had grown into a special woman. She was the right person to be the mother of Jesus.

The Praying Step

Ask God to help you grow into the person He wants you to be.
Thank Him that He has a plan for your life.

Be transformed by the renewing of your mind, that you
may prove what is that good and acceptable and perfect
will of God.

—*Romans 12:2*

The Shepherds: Welcoming God's Son

Luke 2:8–18

The Thinking Step

Have you ever met someone famous or important?
Who is usually invited to meet important people who come to town?

The Reading Step

God's only Son was born in a stable in Bethlehem. An angel in the sky shared the news of Jesus' birth. But the angel did not tell the news to kings or presidents or famous people. The angel told simple shepherds in a field.

The shepherds were afraid of the angel. But the angel said, "Do not be afraid. A Savior is born today in the city of David. He is Christ the Lord!" Then the angel told the shepherds where to find the baby. Angels filled the sky. They praised God that Jesus was born.

The shepherds hurried to Bethlehem to see the baby. They saw Jesus there. Then they went away. The shepherds told everyone the exciting news.

The Praying Step

Thank Jesus for coming to be our Savior.
Thank God that Jesus came for everyone.
Ask God to help you tell others about Jesus.

That which we have seen and heard we declare to you, that you also may have fellowship with us.

—*1 John 1:3*

The Man with the Crippled Hand: Honoring the Lord's Day

Luke 6:1–11

The Thinking Step

God said that one day of the week would be His day.
God's day was called *Sabbath*. It was a day of rest after six days of work.
Today, most Christians call Sunday the day of rest, or the Lord's Day.
How is Sunday different from other days at your house?

The Reading Step

The Pharisees wanted all people to obey God. They made up many rules about how to obey God. They thought all people should obey the rules they made up.

One Sabbath morning, Jesus and His friends went for a walk in a wheat field. Some of the friends broke off the wheat and ate the grains. The Pharisees said Jesus' friends broke the law. But Jesus said He was the Lord of the Sabbath. He made the rules!

On a different Sabbath, a man with a crippled hand went to hear Jesus. The Pharisees did not want Jesus to heal the man. But Jesus healed the man anyway. Jesus said it is right to do good.

The Praying Step

Thank Jesus for this special day each week.
Tell Jesus you want Him to be Lord every day of your life.

This is the day the LORD has made;
We will rejoice and be glad in it.
—*Psalm 118:24*

The Apostles: Saying Yes to Jesus

Luke 6:12–16

The Thinking Step

Have you ever made a hard decision?
Have you ever moved away from family or friends?
How did you feel?

The Reading Step

Jesus had many followers or disciples. They followed Him everywhere He went. One night Jesus went to a mountain. He stayed there all night and prayed.

The next day He called all His disciples to Him. Jesus chose twelve of them to be His apostles. They would be good friends to Him. They would be like His family. The apostles would go from town to town. They would tell people about Jesus. They would be able to heal sick people.

The twelve men all said yes to Jesus. They would have to leave their families and jobs to be with Jesus. But they knew it was the right thing to do.

Jesus was getting them ready to do His work. They became the first missionaries. Many times they faced great danger. But they trusted God.

The Praying Step

Ask God for help to tell someone about Him.
Thank God that He helps us be brave.

You did not choose Me, but I chose you and appointed you that you should go and bear fruit.

—John 15:16

The Centurion: Recognizing Jesus' Authority

Luke 7:1–10

The Thinking Step

What does *authority* mean?
Do you know someone who has authority?
How do other people treat that person?

The Reading Step

Jesus visited the city of Capernaum. One day some people told Jesus about an army officer's problem. This man had a servant that he liked very much. The servant was sick. He might even die. The army officer was a Roman soldier. The Jewish leaders told Jesus that this man deserved Jesus' help.

Jesus started to the officer's house. He went a little way. Then He got a message. It was from the army officer. The officer said that Jesus did not have to come all the way to his house. He knew Jesus had great authority. All Jesus had to do was give an order. Then the man's servant would be well again.

Jesus could not believe it. He said He had never seen a person with so much faith. Jesus gave the order. And the servant was healed instantly!

The Praying Step

Thank the Lord for the authority He has.

Thank Him that you can ask for His help with anything.

> **Whatever you ask in My name, that I will do.**
> —*John 14:13*

Jesus: Teaching His Friends to Pray

Luke 11:1–4

The Thinking Step

Do you know what a pattern is?

Have you seen anyone use a pattern to make clothing?

Have you seen anyone use a pattern to build something?

Jesus gave His friends a pattern for praying!

Think about making a list of people and things to pray about. Think about making a list of answers, too!

The Reading Step

Jesus talked to God often. One day a disciple said to Jesus, "Teach us to pray." Jesus gave the disciples a prayer pattern.

God loves His children. God wants us to ask Him for what we need *each* day. Not all days are the same. Some days we need help with schoolwork. Some days a friend is sick. Some days we cannot find a library book.

Almost always we need to tell God about something.

Almost always we need Him to forgive us.

Almost always we need to forgive other people.

The Praying Step

Thank God for being your Father.
Thank God for hearing you when you talk to Him.
Tell God you want His will to be done.

By prayer and supplication, with thanksgiving, let your requests be made known to God.

—*Philippians 4:6*

The Good Shepherd: Knowing Us by Our Names

Luke 15:3–6; John 10:2–5

The Thinking Step

Did you know Jesus is the Good Shepherd?
How does He care for you?

The Reading Step

Jesus told a story about a shepherd who had one hundred sheep. Every night the shepherd counted his sheep. He wanted to make sure the sheep were all together. One night the shepherd counted and one sheep was missing. That one sheep was important to him. He looked for it right away. And he looked until he found the sheep. Jesus said He is like that shepherd. He came to the world to find people who are lost and need Him.

Jesus also told about a good shepherd. This shepherd knew each of his sheep by name. Jesus said, "The sheep know his voice. They follow him."

Jesus said, "I am the Good Shepherd. I know My sheep, and My sheep know Me." People who love Jesus are His sheep.

The Praying Step

Thank Jesus that He is your Good Shepherd.

Thank Him that He always knows where you are and what is happening to you.

Ask Him to help you hear His voice and follow Him.

> **I know My sheep, and am known by My own.**
> **—*John 10:14***

The Dying Thief: Living Forever with Jesus

Luke 23:39–43

The Thinking Step

Have you asked Jesus to forgive your sins?
Will you be with Him in heaven someday?
Is there any other way that you can get to heaven?

The Reading Step

Some terrible things happened to Jesus. He did nothing wrong. But He was nailed to a cross between two robbers. One of the robbers said unkind things to Him. "If You are really the Christ, save Yourself. Save us, too, while You are at it!"

The other robber heard those unkind words. He thought the first robber was bad. The man looked at Jesus. He knew Jesus was the Son of God. He told Jesus he would like to go to heaven. Jesus kindly said, "You will be with Me in heaven today." Those were the last words Jesus said until it was time for Him to die.

The Praying Step

If you have not done so, ask Jesus to forgive your sins and be your Savior. Thank Him for His promise that we can be in heaven with Him.

> **Believe on the Lord Jesus Christ, and you will be saved.**
> —*Acts 16:31*

John the Baptist: Pointing People to Jesus

John 1:26–29

The Thinking Step

Have you ever introduced two friends to each other?
How would you feel if they became best friends?

The Reading Step

John the Baptist was doing what he wanted to do. He was telling people all about Jesus.

John the Baptist lived in the wilderness. People from nearby cities and villages went to hear him.

One day John preached to a crowd of people. He looked into the crowd and saw Jesus. John shouted to the crowd. He told them Jesus is the "Lamb of God who takes away the sin of the world!"

The next day John talked to two of his followers. He told them that Jesus was the Lamb of God. And John's two followers went to Jesus. That is what John wanted.

The Praying Step

Thank God that someone told you about Jesus.
Ask God to help you tell someone about Him.

He must increase, but I must decrease.   —*John 3:30*

Andrew: Sharing the Good News

John 1:35–42; Acts 2:36–41

The Thinking Step

Who is the first person you tell when you get exciting news?
Does your friend usually share your joy?
Do you know what goes on in heaven when just one person repents?
(Read Luke 15:10.)

The Reading Step

Andrew liked to find out things. John the Baptist pointed to Jesus. John said Jesus was the Lamb of God. Andrew and another man followed Him. They asked, "Where are You staying?" Jesus answered, "Come and see." Andrew spent all day with Him. He asked questions and thought about the answers. The next day Andrew brought his brother Simon to Jesus. Jesus gave Simon a new name—Peter.

Peter became one of Jesus' closest friends.

Three years later Peter spoke to a large crowd. He said, "You killed Jesus. But God made Jesus Lord." They were shocked. They asked, "What should we do?" Peter told them to repent and get baptized. That day 3,000 people believed the message!

We do not hear much more about Andrew. But Peter continued to preach for a long time.

The Praying Step

Tell God the name of someone you want to bring to Jesus.
Ask Him to give you the right words at the right time.

Grow in the grace and knowledge of our Lord and Savior Jesus Christ.

—*2 Peter 3:18*

Mary: Asking for Jesus' Help

John 2:1–10

The Thinking Step

What do you do when you have a problem?
Do you ask Jesus to help?
Does Jesus like to help you?
Do you remember to thank Him?

The Reading Step

Jesus' mother helped with the refreshments at a wedding feast. Everyone enjoyed them. Then the servers saw that they were out of wine.

Jesus lived at home. He worked in the carpenter shop. Perhaps His mother brought her problems to Him. So Mary said to Jesus, "They have no wine." Jesus asked her what that had to do with Him. He meant that from then on the will of God came first. Mary told the servants to do whatever Jesus said to do.

Jesus told the servants to fill six huge stone jars with water. Then He told them to dip some out. They took it to the man in charge of the feast. Often people serve the best wine first. The man tasted the wine. He said to the groom, "You have kept the good wine until now!"

The Praying Step

Ask Jesus' help with a problem you are having.
Thank Him for His help.

Our help is in the name of the LORD,
Who made heaven and earth.
—*Psalm 124:8*

The Woman at the Well: Drinking Living Water

John 4:1–14, 25–29, 39

The Thinking Step

Think about how important water is in our world.
Plants need water to grow. People need water to stay alive.

The Reading Step

Jesus and His disciples were going home to Galilee. They were hot and tired. The disciples went into town to buy food. Jesus sat beside a well and rested. A woman from the village came to the well. She needed to fill her water jar.

Jesus asked the woman for a drink of water. The woman was surprised. Jews did not usually talk to Samaritans. Jesus told her that He could give her special water. She would never be thirsty again. The woman did not believe Him. He did not even have a bucket to get water from the well. Jesus told her that His living water would give her eternal life.

The woman knew someday the Messiah would come. Jesus told her that He was the Messiah. The woman ran back to town. Many people believed in Jesus because of that woman.

The Praying Step

Thank God for giving the water for our plants and trees.
Thank God for the living water that keeps you growing.
Ask Him for strength to share the living water with others.

> He who believes in Me, as the Scripture has said, out of his heart will flow rivers of living water.
>
> *—John 7:38*

Jesus: Satisfying Hungry People

John 6:1–13

The Thinking Step

Does it make you sad when some people do not have food to eat?

Jesus likes it when His friends share food with people who do not have enough to eat.

Hearts can feel hungry, too. What "food" does a hungry heart need?

The Reading Step

Crowds of people followed Jesus. It was time to eat. Jesus and His disciples wanted to be alone. But the crowd hurried to meet them. There were thousands of people!

Jesus asked Philip where they could buy food for so many people. Philip said that it would cost too much to buy food for so many people. Then Andrew told Jesus that a boy wanted to share his food.

The boy had only two small fish and five barley loaves. But Jesus said, "Tell everyone to sit down." Jesus thanked His Father. Jesus gave pieces of bread and fish to the disciples. The disciples gave pieces of bread and fish to the hungry people. And the more people ate, the more food there was.

The Praying Step

Tell Jesus you want to share His love with someone, just like He shared His bread and fish.

> Jesus said to them, "I am the bread of life. He who comes to Me shall never hunger."
>
> —*John 6:35*

Mary and Martha: Knowing God's Comfort

John 11:32–44

The Thinking Step

Has someone you cared about died?
How did you feel?
Did you wish you could be with that person again?

The Reading Step

Mary and Martha were sad. Their brother Lazarus had died. Jesus was sad, too. Lazarus was His friend. Mary and Martha knew that Jesus could have kept Lazarus alive.

Something wonderful happened. Jesus told Mary and Martha that He is the One who can bring dead people back to life. Mary and Martha believed Jesus is the Son of God. They knew He could do wonderful things.

Jesus, Mary, Martha, and their friends went to the tomb. This was where Lazarus was buried. Jesus said, "Take the stone away from the door." Then He called, "Lazarus, come out!" Everyone wondered what He meant. Lazarus had been dead four days. But Lazarus walked out of his tomb! He was wrapped in the burial clothes. But he was alive! Jesus said, "Loose him, and let him go." Everyone was happy.

The Praying Step

If you are sad about something, tell God about it.
Thank God that He cares when we feel bad.
Ask Him to comfort someone you know who is hurting today.

[God] comforts us in all our tribulation.
—*2 Corinthians 1:4*

Mary Magdalene: Telling the Good News

John 20:1–18

The Thinking Step

Have you ever lost a good friend?
How did you feel?

The Reading Step

Mary was sad when Jesus died. Jesus was her best friend.

It was early the day after Jesus was buried. Mary went to His tomb. She saw that the stone blocking the door was rolled away. Jesus' body was gone! Mary ran to tell Peter and another disciple. Later, Mary stood near the tomb and cried. Then she saw two angels inside. They asked her why she was crying. Mary told them that Jesus' body was gone. She thought someone stole it.

Mary turned to leave. She saw a man standing nearby. Mary thought the man was the caretaker of the tomb. She asked where Jesus' body was.

The man said, "Mary." Suddenly Mary knew the man was not a caretaker. He was Jesus! She was happy! Jesus gave her a message for His disciples. So she ran to tell them that He was alive!

The Praying Step

Thank God that Jesus is alive.
Thank Him for His love.
Ask Him to help you tell others the good news.

He is not here, but is risen!   —*Luke 24:6*

Peter and John: Giving What You Have

Acts 3:1–11, 16

The Thinking Step

What is the best gift you ever received?
What is the best gift you ever gave?
Do you wish you could give someone a really wonderful gift?

The Reading Step

Peter and John were going to the temple to pray. They saw some men carrying another man. The man could not walk. He had never been able to walk. His friends carried him to the temple gate every day. He begged for money from the people who went by.

Peter and John went up to the man. The man asked them for some money. Peter and John looked right at the man. They did not have money to give him. They had something much better. Peter called on the name of Jesus. He told the man to get up and walk.

The man's feet and ankles were healed instantly! He jumped for joy! He walked into the temple. He shouted praise to God! People in the temple saw who was shouting. They could not believe it. Peter and John told everyone that the power of Jesus' name made the man well.

The Praying Step

Thank God for the gifts He has given you.

Ask God to show you the gifts of kindness and love to others.

If anyone is in Christ, he is a new creation; old things have passed away; behold, all things have become new.

—2 Corinthians 5:17

Peter and John: Honoring the Name of Jesus

Acts 4:1–22

The Thinking Step

Is God at work in your life?

Can people see God at work in your life?

How do you honor Jesus' name?

The Reading Step

At least 5,000 people believed in Jesus. This worried the religious leaders who had helped to crucify Him. The religious leaders put Peter and John in jail. The next morning a man who had been healed stood beside them. Peter and John said that the man was healed by the power of Jesus' name.

The leaders could see the man was healed. But they did not know what to do with Peter and John. They told Peter and John not to speak the name of Jesus again.

Peter and John said that they could not help but talk about the things they saw and heard.

The Praying Step

Thank God that He gave His Son the name Jesus. For Jesus "will save His people from their sins."

Ask God to keep working in your life.

> **There is no other name under heaven given among men by which we must be saved.**
>
> —*Acts 4:12*

The Apostles: Witnessing for Jesus

Acts 5:17–32

The Thinking Step

Witnesses testify (tell the truth) about what they saw or heard.
Why would anyone want to keep a witness quiet?

The Reading Step

The apostles talked about Jesus' resurrection. Large crowds went to hear them. Many people believed. The religious leaders of the city were angry. They put the apostles in jail. But an angel opened the prison doors and let them out. He told them to keep witnessing for Jesus.

In the morning the officers went to get the apostles. They found the prison doors locked. Guards were by the doors. But no one was inside the prison. The officers told the religious leaders about this. Then someone saw the apostles. They were teaching in the temple again.

The officers brought the apostles to the angry leaders. "We told you not to teach in Jesus' name," the high priest said. The high priest claimed the apostles spread bad ideas. He said that the apostles blamed the leaders for Jesus' death. The apostles told the high priest that they obeyed God.

The Praying Step

Thank Jesus for giving His life for us.

Ask Him to give us opportunities and courage to tell others how much we love Him.

> My lips shall utter praise. . . .
> My tongue shall speak of Your word.
> —*Psalm 119:171–172*

Gamaliel: Giving Wise Advice

Acts 5:33–41

The Thinking Step

What does *advice* mean?

Do you know someone who gives good advice?

Does God's Word give advice on how we should live?

The Reading Step

The religious leaders of Jerusalem—the members of the council—were mad. They were ready to kill the apostles. Gamaliel was one of the council members. He was an expert in religious matters.

Gamaliel stood up to speak. Everyone listened with respect. He told the council about two men. The two men tried to get people to follow their ideas. Both men failed.

Gamaliel told the others not to harm the apostles. He said the apostles would fail without God. And if God was on the apostles' side, they could not be stopped.

The council took Gamaliel's advice. They did not kill the apostles. They beat the apostles. They told them not to speak in the name of Jesus. Then they let them go. The apostles left the council room happy. They were proud to suffer for Jesus' name. And they continued to teach and preach every day.

The Praying Step

Thank God for parents or pastors who give good advice.
Thank Him for His word that is full of advice.

Forever, O LORD,
Your word is settled in heaven.
—*Psalm 119:89*

Stephen: Seeing Jesus

Acts 6:8–15; 7:51–60

The Thinking Step

Have you ever wondered what heaven is like?
Do you wish you could see Jesus with your own eyes?

The Reading Step

Jesus' enemies were powerful. But still Stephen told about his faith. He was wise and brave. Jesus' enemies accused Stephen of saying wicked things. Stephen was arrested and brought to the council. And his face was like an angel's face.

Stephen did not defend himself against the lies. He told the council that their people always rejected God. They even killed His prophets. Stephen said they crucified God's own Son, Jesus.

The men got angry. They ground their teeth in rage.

But Stephen told them he saw heaven. He said he saw Jesus at the right hand of God! Stephen's enemies shouted. They dragged Stephen out of the city. Then they threw stones at him to kill him. Stephen prayed, "Lord Jesus, receive my spirit." Then he cried out, "Lord, do not charge them with this sin." And he went to be with Jesus.

The Praying Step

Thank the Lord that He has made heaven so wonderful that you can't imagine what it is like.

Thank Him that Jesus is with us now and will be with us always.

Eye has not seen, nor ear heard, nor have entered into the heart of man the things which God has prepared for those who love Him.

—*1 Corinthians 2:9*

Philip: Keeping an Appointment with God

Acts 8:26–39

The Thinking Step

Have you ever turned a corner and run into someone?
Do you think God ever plans such "appointments"?

The Reading Step

The Ethiopian man was important. He served Ethiopia's queen. The man rode home from Jerusalem in his chariot. And he read aloud from the prophecy of Isaiah. He read about someone who was killed. Isaiah said this person was like a sheep. He did not fight those who killed him.

Philip saw the chariot. He ran to catch up with it. "Do you understand what you read?" Philip asked. The man said he needed help to understand the passage. He invited Philip to sit with him. The man asked who the person in the passage was. Was it Isaiah or someone else? Philip began with that Scripture (Isaiah 53:7–8). He talked to the Ethiopian about Jesus. The Ethiopian believed. He stopped the chariot so Philip could baptize him!

The Praying Step

Tell God you want to fit in with His plans.
Ask Him to help you trust and obey.

> **Always be ready to give a defense to everyone who asks you a reason for the hope that is in you.**
>
> **—*1 Peter 3:15***

Peter: Believing That God Answers Prayer

Acts 12:1–17

The Thinking Step

Do other people pray for you?

Does it make you feel good to know other people pray for you?

Have you ever been surprised that you got something you wanted?

How has God surprised you?

The Reading Step

The first Christians had a very hard time. James was killed because of his faith. Then Peter was made a prisoner. But the church prayed for him constantly.

One night an angel of the Lord went to Peter's cell. The angel told him to get up. When Peter got up, the chains fell off his wrists. The angel led Peter past the guards and out of prison.

Peter knew God set him free. Peter went to see his friends. He knocked at the gate. But his friends could not believe that Peter was free. Peter knocked again and again. At last his friends opened the door. They were happy!

The Praying Step

Thank God for helping you, caring for you, and keeping you safe.
Try to pay attention to how God answers your prayers.

> You will keep him in perfect peace,
> Whose mind is stayed on You,
> Because he trusts in You.
> —*Isaiah 26:3*

John Mark: Being Given a Second Chance

Acts 12:25; 13:5, 13; 15:36–40

The Thinking Step

Have you ever done something wrong or not done something you should have?

Would it help more for someone to show you your mistake or help you start over?

The Reading Step

Paul and Barnabas began their first missionary trip to Cyprus. They took young John Mark with them to help. After a while Mark decided to go home.

Paul and Barnabas finished their trip. They returned to Antioch. They taught and preached in the church. Then Paul told Barnabas they should go see the new Christians in the cities they visited. Barnabas thought it was a good idea. He wanted to take Mark with them again. Paul did not want to take Mark. So the two friends decided to split up. Paul took Silas with him. Barnabas took Mark.

Barnabas gave Mark another chance. Mark did well. He won back Paul's trust.

The Praying Step

Thank the Lord that He forgives us and forgets our mistakes.
Remember that each day with Him is a new start!

As far as the east is from the west,
So far has He removed our transgressions from us.
—*Psalm 103:12*

Paul and Barnabas: Being Chosen

Acts 13:1–5

The Thinking Step

Have you ever been the last one picked to play on a team? How did it feel?

Did you know that each of us is always God's first choice?

The Reading Step

The people in Antioch thought it was all right for others to believe as they chose. So they welcomed new believers in Christ. The believers came from Jerusalem to escape danger.

God sent many preachers and teachers to Antioch. The Christians grew strong in their faith. One day God told the church leaders that He had chosen Barnabas and Saul to do a special kind of work for Him. The leaders gave their blessing. Then Barnabas and Saul (who is also called Paul) left. They sailed to the island of Cyprus.

For twenty years Paul traveled. He visited big cities and small towns. He preached in synagogues and town halls and people's homes. He spoke in palaces and prisons, in desert places and on riverbanks. He talked to kings, governors, soldiers, and merchants. And he never forgot the work God chose him to do.

The Praying Step

Thank the Lord you are His first choice!
Ask God to show you what He wants you to do.

You did not choose Me, but I chose you!
—*John 15:16*

Paul and Barnabas: Giving Glory to God

Acts 14:8–18

The Thinking Step

When has someone made you feel special?
What did you do?
Who is the most special one of all?
How can you make God feel special?

The Reading Step

Paul and Barnabas were missionaries. A missionary is someone who tells other people about Jesus. A missionary sometimes travels a long way to talk to people who have never heard about Jesus.

Paul and Barnabas spoke God's special message. God wanted people to know that. So God helped Paul and Barnabas do things other people could not do. The people were amazed. But they thought that Paul and Barnabas were gods.

"No!" Paul yelled at the people. "We are not gods. We are people just like you. But you should worship the God we worship. He is the one true God." Paul and Barnabas wanted the people to worship God, not them.

146

The Praying Step

Ask God to help you tell your friends about Jesus.
Ask God to help you give Him glory for the things He does.

You shall worship the LORD your God. —*Luke 4:8*

Paul: Standing Firm

Acts 14:19–22

The Thinking Step

Did you know that many people have gone to prison and even died for spreading the gospel?

Did you know that in some places Christians are not allowed to go to church, have a Bible, or tell friends about Jesus?

The Reading Step

Paul and his missionary friends traveled around preaching. Enemies of the gospel tried to stop them any way they could. Some troublemakers from Antioch and Iconium followed Paul to the city of Lystra. There crowds of people listened to Paul.

Soon the troublemakers got these listeners angry at Paul. People picked up stones and threw them at Paul. They dragged him outside the city.

They thought he was dead. The Christians gathered around him. Paul was able to get to his feet.

The next day, Paul went to the town of Derbe. He and Barnabas preached the gospel. Many people believed. Later they went back to Lystra and the troublemakers' hometowns. They told Christians not to give up. They told them to stand firm when others hurt them for believing in Jesus.

The Praying Step

Pray for people who have not heard the gospel yet.
Pray for Christians who have to worship in secret.

Be steadfast, immovable, always abounding in the work of the Lord.

—*1 Corinthians 15:58*

Timothy: Learning Not to Be Afraid

Acts 16:1–3; 1 Thessalonians 3:1–3; 2 Timothy 1:1–8

The Thinking Step

What kinds of things scare you?
What do you do when you are scared?
What makes you feel better?

The Reading Step

Timothy was a little boy. He heard about Jesus. His mother and grandmother taught him stories from the Bible.

One time Paul went to Timothy's church. Paul traveled around a lot. He told people about Jesus. Timothy's friends told Paul that Timothy was a good person. Paul needed a helper. Paul asked Timothy to be his helper. Later he sent Timothy to a town called Thessalonica to help new Christians. This was an important job.

Timothy did a good job. But he was not very brave when he was alone. Paul was put in prison. Timothy got scared. He did not know what would happen. Paul wanted to help Timothy. He wrote letters to him. Those letters are in our Bible now.

One letter Paul wrote said that fear does not come from God. God wants us to be strong and loving. Timothy could be strong. He had Jesus to help him.

The Praying Step

Tell God what scares you.

Ask Him to help you remember that He will help you.

Thank God that He is always with you.

> God has not given us a spirit of fear, but of power and of love and of a sound mind.
>
> —*2 Timothy 1:7*

Apollos: Learning from Other People

Acts 18:1–3, 24–28

The Thinking Step

Do you know people who think they know everything?
Do you enjoy being with them?

The Reading Step

Apollos lived in Alexandria. He was a good Bible teacher. Apollos studied hard.

Apollos heard about John the Baptist. John told people to turn away from their sins. John baptized people so they would be ready for the Messiah. Then Apollos heard about Jesus. Apollos believed Jesus was the Messiah because of all the things Jesus had done.

Apollos went to Ephesus. He taught in the synagogue or church. He told people there that Jesus was really the Messiah.

Aquila and Priscilla heard Apollos speak. They knew that Apollos did not know the whole story about Jesus. Aquila and Priscilla invited Apollos to their home. They told him how Jesus died, rose from the dead, and went back to heaven. Then Apollos knew the whole story. He was glad Aquila and Priscilla took the time to tell him.

The Praying Step

Tell God you want to learn more about Him.
Ask Him to help you teach others about His love.

Open my eyes, that I may see
Wondrous things from Your law.
—*Psalm 119:18*

Eutychus: Being Hungry for God's Word

Acts 20:7–12

The Thinking Step

Have you ever felt sleepy or hungry during a long sermon?
What kind of hunger did the early Christians have?

The Reading Step

The first Christians were hungry for the gospel. It was all so new. There was so much to learn.

Paul preached and taught for a week at Troas. Paul was leaving on Monday. On Sunday the people wanted him to keep on preaching. And he did. He preached long past lunchtime and even supper time. In fact, he preached until midnight!

Everybody was crowded into an upstairs room. The oil lamps gave off a smoky, dim light. The room got stuffy. A young man named Eutychus sat on a windowsill. He kept dozing off. Finally he went sound asleep. He fell three stories to the ground!

Paul ran down to check on him. He told the Christians, "Don't worry. He is all right." They all went back upstairs. And Paul preached until the sun came up the next morning.

The Praying Step

Thank God for "daily bread" that keeps us strong and well.
Ask Him to fill our hearts and minds with His word so that we can be
His healthy children.

I am the bread of life. He who comes to Me shall never
hunger.

—John 6:35

Paul: Traveling with the Gospel

Acts 20:17–24

The Thinking Step

Can you find Israel on a map? Can you find Syria? Can you find Turkey? Can you find Greece? Can you find Italy?

Paul traveled to all these places. He wanted to tell people about Jesus.

The Reading Step

It was not easy for people to travel in Paul's day. Most people walked or rode donkeys or horses. They had to watch out for robbers. Some people traveled by boat. They had to watch out for storms.

Paul was shipwrecked three times. He was beaten. He was put in jail. People who did not like Jesus did not like Paul.

But many people listened to what Paul said. Some decided they believed in Jesus. They became Christians. When Paul traveled, he wrote letters to the new Christians. Even when Paul was in prison, he wrote letters to the new Christians.

Paul said that being in prison did not bother him. He said that God was more important.

The Praying Step

Thank God for missionaries, the people who travel to other places and tell people about Jesus.

Pray for one missionary family that you know of.

> For I am not ashamed of the gospel of Christ, for it is the power of God to salvation.
>
> *—Romans 1:16*

The Apostle Paul: Being Committed to Jesus

Acts 21:1–14

The Thinking Step

Has someone ever asked you to do something difficult?
Did you do it? Why or why not?

The Reading Step

The apostle Paul loved Jesus very much. He told people about Jesus for many years. Paul wanted everyone to love Jesus as much as he did.

Paul wanted to go to Jerusalem. Jerusalem is an important city in Israel. Paul wanted to tell the people in Jerusalem about Jesus. Paul stopped to see some Christian friends on his way to Jerusalem. At one place Agabus talked to Paul. Agabus had a special message for Paul.

He took off Paul's belt. He tied Paul's hands and feet. Then he said to Paul, "This is what will happen to you if you go to Jerusalem."

Paul's friends begged Paul not to go to Jerusalem. But Paul would not listen. "Why do you say this?" Paul asked. "I will do whatever God wants because I love Jesus."

158

The Praying Step

Ask God to help you be committed to Him.
Ask God to help you be brave enough to obey Him always.

You shall love the LORD your God with all your heart,
with all your soul, and with all your strength.
—*Deuteronomy 6:5*